The Battle of

Towton

1461

Leonard James

Acknowledgements

Photos, illustrations and maps are by the author except:
Bridge Street Pontefract, Rept0n1x; Oddfellows Arms, Tim Green;
Drawings by Leanne Goodall and Darren Bennett.

Website - www.BretwaldaBooks.com
Twitter - @Bretwaldabooks
Facebook - Bretwalda Books
Blog - bretwaldabooks.blogspot.co.uk/

Bretwalda Books
Unit 8, Fir Tree Close, Epsom,
Surrey KT17 3LD
info@BretwaldaBooks.com
www.BretwaldaBooks.com
ISBN 978-1-909698-90-1

CONTENTS

Chapter 1
The Wars of the Roses

The civil wars that tore England apart in the later 15th century are known to historians as the Wars of Roses, since the two factions chose different coloured roses among their symbols - white for York and red for Lancaster. Although the background to the wars was complex and the shifting allegiances of the fighters is often difficult to follow, the main issue at stake was simple: What should be done if the king was incapable of competent rule?

By this date the person who sat on the throne of England was determined by strict rules of primogeniture. The eldest son of the previous monarch became king. If there was no son, the eldest daughter became queen. If there were no children than a younger brother took over, or if he had died, his children. The advantages of the system are clear: There could be no dispute over who should be the next monarch and so no disagreements that might lead to civil war.

The system of primogeniture had been growing increasingly important, but had been cemented in 1216 when King Henry III took over from his father King John despite being aged only nine years old at the time. The formal proclamation of Henry's right to the kingship mentioned only that he was the oldest son of the previous king.

At the same time the reigning monarch was expected to lead the government of the kingdom in a very real way. It was the king who made all the big decisions, and the king who appointed officials to look after less important issues. The king could appoint who he liked, and sack them if they did not act as he wished. Such autocratic power had long been less impressive than in theory it seemed.

Since Magna Carta was agreed in 1215 the monarch had been obliged to obey the law of the land, and he had always been expected to take into account the views and opinions of his nobles and the Church. Increasingly the monarch also had to listen to the views of the richer commoners, who elected men to sit in Parliament and who had to agree before any new tax could be levied. Nevertheless, the king was the most powerful man in the kingdom and while he

4

had to listen to others, the final decision was his.

What nobody seems to have considered was what should happen if the King of England was incapable of making decisions. In an earlier age unsuitable monarchs were dealt with crudely - In 1327 Edward II had been murdered on the orders of his wife and a gang of senior noblemen - but by the later 15th century such brutal acts were no longer possible. The law had to be obeyed.

The problem was forced into sharp focus in 1453 when King Henry VI had a mental breakdown and was simply incapable of making any decisions. The nobles called a Great Council to consider what should be done, and appointed the king's cousin Richard, Duke of York, to be Protector of the Realm. York was effectively

King Henry VI reigned from 1422 when he inherited the throne at the age of just nine months. He grew up to be a weak, indecisive man who suffered episodes of mental illness. His inability to keep a firm grip on government led to the Wars of the Roses.

5

given the powers of the king until such time as Henry should regain his sense. York proved to be far more efficient, effective and competent than Henry VI had been. After years of growing injustice, corruption and tyranny, England suddenly experienced a bout of good government.

In January 1455 Henry recovered his sense and retook the reins of power. At once he reversed nearly everything York had achieved. Corrupt officials who York had sacked were reinstated, feuds were revived and justice again denied the people. The English nobles and the richer commoners were in a dilemma. Henry was the anointed king, but York was the better ruler.

Those returning to power, led by Henry's wife Queen Margaret and her favourite, the Duke of Somerset, were determined to get revenge on York and the barons who had supported him - especially the Duke of Salisbury and the Earl of Warwick from the rich and talented Neville family. In April 1455 York, Salisbury and Warwick mustered a body of armed men and set out to see the king, justifying their army on the grounds they feared that they would be murdered by Somerset's men.

The two bodies of men clashed at St Albans on 22 May in what historians have dignified with the title First Battle of St Albans, but which was in fact more of a vicious armed brawl. Somerset was killed along with several of his supporters and Henry was captured by York. Henry promptly had another breakdown and York was again appointed temporary ruler. Efforts were made to smooth over the quarrel and find a compromise by which everyone could abide, but too many men nursed a desire for revenge for relatives killed at St Albans, and Queen Margaret was doing everything she could to return herself to power.

In April 1459 Margaret summoned a Great Council to meet. She did not invite York, Salisbury or Warwick and told those she did invite to "bring as many men defensibly arrayed as they might and to bring with them expenses for 2 months." It was a summons to civil war. York fled to Ireland with his second son the Earl of Rutland while Salisbury, Warwick and York's first son Edward Earl of March went to France.

What everybody knew, but so far nobody had said, was that the entire issue was complicated by a dynastic dispute that had taken place 50 years earlier. When Richard II abdicated he had been replaced by his cousin Henry, Duke of Lancaster who thus became King Henry IV, grandfather to Henry VI. However, there had been another cousin who was overlooked as being too young and inexperienced to become king. That cousin had sensibly kept his head down when he grew up, and then had died young. However, his great grandson was none other than Richard, Duke of York. When it came to claims to the throne, York had arguably a better claim than did Henry VI himself.

In the summer of 1460 the Yorkist earls returned to England. They defeated a hastily gathered army of Lancastrians loyal to Henry VI at Northampton. In October a new Parliament was summoned. Henry was too ill to attend, but York

A Victorian view of the incident in the Temple Garden, London, when nobles picked roses to indicate which side they supported in the dispute between York and Lancaster.

7

put before it a host of new legislation and measures, all of which were passed without much argument.

Bouyed up by success, York then claimed the throne for himself. There was a deathly silence in Parliament. Most people wanted York to head the government, but very few wanted to get rid of Henry. Parliament decided that succession to the throne was a matter for the Lords. The Lords said it was a matter of law and turned to the assembled Justices. The Justices decided to consult a convocation of lawyers on a point of law. The lawyers fled without giving an answer. York demanded an answer from the Lords, who fudged by deciding that Henry would remain King of England, but that when he died York would inherit.

That drove to fury Queen Margaret as it meant that her son by King Henry was disinherited and she herself permanently excluded from power. She at once began mustering an army as secretly as she could. The Duke of York and Earl of Salisbury were lured into a trap by the new Duke of Somerset at the Battle of Wakefield and killed. The Earl of Warwick was defeated at St Albans, although he managed to get most of his army away intact.

That left Edward, who was now the new Duke of York, with an army in western England. He defeated a small Lancastrian force sent against him at the Battle of Mortimer's Cross, then marched to London to join with Warwick. As Edward entered London he was greeted by cheering crowds chanting the name of "King Edward". Young Edward consulted the lords and rich merchants who were in London and then in Westminster Hall he was hailed as King of England by Warwick. Heralds read out his claim to the throne based on descent from King Edward III, and Henry VI was declared to be an illegitimate king. Cheering broke out again.

But nobody was under any illusions. Margaret and Somerset were in northern England mustering the largest army that England had ever seen. If he were to make his claim to the throne a reality, Edward would have to defeat them. On 16 March Edward rode out of London and headed north. He was on a road that would lead to Towton.

Chapter 2
Commanders at Towton

The vast Lancastrian army that fought at Towton was nominally under the command of King Henry VI, though in fact he was in no fit state to be in charge of anything. He was aged 40 by this date and had already suffered several bouts of mental breakdown and periods of temporary insanity. When in his right mind Henry preferred to spend time in church or organising artistic or educational projects. His sole known contribution to the Towton campaign was to instruct the Duke of Somerset not to fight a battle on Palm Sunday - an instruction Somerset promptly ignored.

It was Henry Beaufort, Duke of Somerset, who seems to have been the most senior of the Lancastrian commanders in the campaign. It is clear, however, that his right to command was not undisputed and the other senior Lancastrians seem to have considered themselves free to act pretty much as they liked.

Somerset was 25 years old at the time of the battle, and already a seasoned military commander. Like all late medieval noblemen he had been brought up expecting to go to war at some point and had been taught how to use swords, lances and other weapons of war as a part of his youthful education. Being born into one of the country's premier noble families - the Beauforts were descended from King Edward III's third son John of Gaunt - he had also been trained in the skills necessary to command an army. His father, also Duke of Somerset, had been a leading member of the Lancastrian faction from the very earliest days of the disputes that led to the Wars of the Roses. Young Somerset followed his father to St Albans in 1455 and took part in the battle there. The elder Somerset was killed in the fighting and the younger man was wounded. He recovered from his wounds and took his father's place as a leading Lancastrian.

There was no doubting either his courage or his military skill. At the Battle of Wakefield in 1460 he cleverly misled the Duke of York as to the true strength of the Lancastrian force and lured him into a rash advance that ended in disaster for the Yorkists, and death for York himself. The following year he commanded again

9

at the Second Battle of St Albans. There he used a wide outflanking manoeuver to defeat the Earl of Warwick. Commanders such as Somerset were quite capable of moving large bodies of men around in surprisingly complex manoeuvres, belying the popular image of medieval battles as being brutal, simple, slogging matches.

There can be no doubt that on the eve of the Battle of Towton, Somerset was the most widely respected of all the commanders present, though as we will see Fauconberg on the Yorkist side would have run him a close second.

A very different character was John Clifford, 9th Baron de Clifford, who was possibly the most unpopular man in England - even his fellow Lancastrians seem not to have liked him. He was vicious and a killer, who had earned the nickname of "Butcher" long before the Towton campaign.

His most notorious act came in the wake of the Battle of Wakefield, where he commanded the left wing of Somerset's Lancastrian army. The Lancastrians had won the day and the Yorkists were being rounded up when Clifford's men found young Edmund Plantagenet, Earl of Rutland, on Wakefield Bridge. Rutland was the Duke of York's second son and as well as being a youth had played no part in

The murder of the youthful Earl of Rutland on the bridge at Wakefield a few weeks before the Battle of Towton made Lord Clifford one of the most hated men in England. He knew that he could expect no mercy from Rutland's elder brother, Edward IV, when the two met in battle at Towton.

the battle. By the rules of war of the time - even of civil war - Rutland should have been taken prisoner. Clifford's men were holding the boy, but Clifford dragged him aside with obviously murderous intent. A priest leapt forward shouting "Save him", but Clifford punched the priest to the ground, then drew his dagger and stabbed Rutland to death. Rutland's head, as well as that of the Duke of York, were then chopped off and displayed on spikes over the gates of York, where they still stood as the armies gathered at Towton.

Henry Percy, Earl of Northumberland, was aged 40 at the time of the campaign and was one of the richest men in England. He sided with the Lancastrians not out of any real commitment to the cause of Henry VI, but more because it allowed him to carry on his feud with the Neville family who supported the Duke of York. He commanded a division at the Battle of Wakefield in 1460, but otherwise was not especially experienced in actual battle - though he had on many occasions led men on campaign.

Randolph Dacre, Baron Dacre, was a younger son of Baron Thomas Dacre who lived at Naworth Castle and was one of the greatest landowners in

King Edward IV was firmly in command of the Yorkist army at the Battle of Towton. At the time, however, he was only 19 years old but had already fought in several battles. It is clear, however, that he relied for advice on his older and more experienced comrades, the Earl of Warwick and Baron Fauconberg, though not so much as in earlier battles. His personal courage and leadership would prove to be critical at the turning point in the Battle of Towton.

northwestern England. He is not mentioned much by contemporary chroniclers, and is notable mostly for the manner of his death.

Thomas Courtenay, Earl of Devon, was the fourteenth member of his family to hold the earldom and through his mother was a great grandson of King Edward III. Like Clifford, Exeter liked to settle disputes by violence. Even before the Wars of the Roses began he had murdered a neighbouring landowner and burned the houses of two others. He was a notoriously violent man who urged Somerset not to take prisoners at Wakefield, and supported Clifford over the killing of Rutland.

The Yorkist army was commanded by the 19 year old King Edward IV. Tall, blond and handsome, Edward was the very picture of a dashing medieval king. At the time of this campaign, however, he had only recently stepped out from the shadow of his father, Richard Duke of York, who had been killed at the Battle of Wakefield. Edward had realised that he could not trust the Lancastrians to stick to any agreements they made and so had claimed the title of king in order to push the war to a conclusion. He was a very popular young prince who had already shown himself to be charming, intelligent and politically astute.

As a military commander, Edward had fought at the Battle of Northampton in 1460 and at Mortimer's Cross earlier in 1461. However in the first battle he had served under the Earl of Warwick and in the second had enjoyed a clear superiority of numbers. His skills as a commander were, therefore, relatively unknown.

Richard Neville, Earl of Warwick, was 33 years old and had a reputation as a consummate politician and military commander. It had largely been because of Warwick's support that the powerful Neville family had declared for the Duke of York and it was Warwick's contacts that largely ensured that so many men mustered on the Yorkist side at Towton. He had fought at the First Battle of St Albans, Blore Heath and at Ludford Bridge. He commanded at Northampton, where he won, and at Second St Albans, where he lost. He was certainly experienced as a military commander, but his record was a mixed one.

More experienced and most successful than either Edward or Warwick, though junior to them in rank, was William Neville, Baron Fauconberg. Fauconberg was 55 years old at Towton and was uncle to Warwick on his father's side. His title came through marriage to Joan Fauconberg, one of the wealthiest heiresses in northern England at the time of their marriage in 1422. In the 1430s he fought in several campaigns in France, at one point alongside Richard, Duke of York, and enjoyed much success, especially at siege warfare. In 1443 he moved to Roxburgh Castle from where he commanded the English forces along the Scottish border. Six years later he returned to France and was captured in a crafty ambush by the French. The skirmish was enlivened by Fauconberg's refusal to surrender to anyone other than a lord. He fought manfully against overwhelming odds, being almost killed at one point, until a French lord appeared.

When the Wars of the Roses broke out, Fauconberg sided with his old commander the Duke of York. This was partly because he admired York and partly because Henry VI had refused to honour a debt of £1,000 owed to Fauconberg for work he had done on the Scottish borders.

John Mowbray, Duke of Norfolk, was aged 46 at Towton and was another veteran of the wars in France. His military experience was not extensive and had been largely restricted to garrison duty and to mustering troops for campaigns that never took place. He fought under Warwick at the Second Battle of St Albans and was largely instrumental in organising the rearguard during the retreat, thus allowing most of the Yorkist troops to escape the defeat.

Richard Neville, 16th Earl of Warwick, as shown in the Rous Roll. This document was drawn up by John Rous in about 1483 and is a major source for history of the period of the Wars of the Roses. Rous presents a highly biased pro-Yorkist view of the wars. In 1460 Warwick was one of the richest and most influential noblemen in England, though many older noblemen regarded him as something of an upstart.

Chapter 3
Men, Weapons and Tactics

The armies of the Wars of the Roses were raised in three basic ways. First there were the town and county militias, second were the retainers of the various noblemen and third were mercenaries, mostly foreigners. The town and county militias in the 15th century were the descendants of the old feudal levy. Each town and city was expected to have a full time guard which patrolled the city walls, secured the city gates at night and kept order on the streets. The men would also guard the gates during the day, collecting any tolls that were due from merchants and keeping an eye open for undesirables. These men might number only a dozen or so and were employed full time by the council, their equipment, food and lodging usually being provided.

There was also the militia, sometimes termed "trained bands", made up of citizens who were trained to use weapons at weekends, but who worked at their own trades during the week. Arrangements varied, but these men were usually paid a small amount each month in return for turning up to train equipped with weapons and armour. Each town or county employed a Constable who was responsible for training the men, checking their equipment and recording any absences from training sessions. In times of war he was the commander of the unit on campaign.

The militia were under the control of the crown and so were expected to be loyal to the reigning monarch. This was part of the military set up that for centuries had made England far less prone to rebellions and civil wars than other European states. With so much of the military apparatus in the hands of the monarch, it was a brave nobleman indeed who started an armed rebellion. However, by the time of Towton there were two men claiming to be the King of England. This put the local authorities in a quandary. If they answered one call for soldiers, they might find themselves accused of treason by the other.

In the spring of 1461 Norwich received a commission of array from Queen Margaret in the name of King Henry VI. The commission demanded 120 fully

14

equiped infantry to fight against rebels and traitors. Norwich city council complied promptly enough, getting volunteers together, providing them with campaigning suits of clothes and checking over their arms and armour. But before the 120 men set off they held a meeting in front of the cathedral. After some discussion the men decided that they favoured the Yorkist cause, and so marched to fight against Margaret instead of for her. The council was, apparently, not consulted and the decision made by the men themselves.

If details of the militia are rather scarce, we know rather more about the retainers as this system involved cash changing hands for written contracts, called indentures, some of which have survived.

Rates of pay varied, but the average for the mid 15th century was for an archer to get three pennies a day, a hobilar six pennies, a man at arms one shilling, a knight two shillings a knight banneret four shillings and a nobleman six shillings and eight pennies. There was usually a "regard" paid at the end of the contract, assuming that the men had performed their duties well. This might be as much as the value of the contract, but was usually less. All pay was in cash and if the pay fell into arrears the men were entitled to go home before the contract ended.

The ratios between the different types of man also varied, but by 1450 it was usual for there to be five or six archers for each man at arms, three or four men at arms for each knight (nobles counting as knights for this purpose). The size of indentures varied wildly with individual knights agreeing a contract to come along in person along with half a dozen archers, while the famous commanders might agree to provide up to 4,000 men. Interestingly the numbers of men a commander

This hobilar, or pricker, is typical of Wars of the Roses cavalry. He wears a helmet of metal padded with wool. His leather sleeveless jack has overlapping metal plates and is worn over a mail shirt that reaches to the elbows and to mid-thigh. His leg armour is made of plate and covers him from upper thigh to toe. For weapons he has a long but light lance, backed by a sword. Such men had many uses on campaign, but few on the battlefield.

could put together bore no relation to his social rank. The Earl of Devon could muster only 110 men, while Sir Robert Knollys, a mere knight, could regularly field over 3,000 men. It was fame and competence that enabled a man to attract followers, not wealth or rank. As a rule the same men served under the same commander year after year.

Artillery were also to be seen on battlefields during the Wars of the Roses, manned by either foreign mercenaries or English gunners. The really big cannon, bombards able to hurl stones weighing stones weighing 200lb, were not seen on battlefields. They were massively expensive to make, difficult to transport and virtually immobile on the battlefield. Essential in sieges, they were simply too big and heavy for battles. Battlefield artillery went by a variety of names, though culverine and serpentine seem to have been popular. These guns had barrels about eight to 12 feet long and fired stone or iron shot weighing about 10 to 20lb. The cannon were mounted on carriages that had two large wheels and a long wooden trail behind. The trail was used to pull the gun around the battlefiled, or swivel it from side to side before firing. The barrel could be raised or lowered with a wooden wedge to alter the range. On the move the trail was fixed to a cart containing the ammunition and pulled by oxen or horses. There was usually at least one other cart filled with ammunition.

What all these guns and firearms had in common was their complete

This archer is typical of the period. Because large numbers of archers served on both sides he is wearing fairly substantial armour to provide protection against incoming arrows. He has a mail shirt reaching to elbows and knees. Over this he wears a sleeveless jack made of up to 22 layers of linen over which are stitched plates of iron or horn. His sallet-style helmet is of steel, padded with wool. His lower arms are free to allow him to draw his bow. The lower legs are unarmoured, probably to allow him to move nimbly around the battlefield. His bow is the standard longbow of the period and he has a quiver of arrows at his belt. His sword and buckler are for hand to hand fighting.

16

unpredictability. Even in the hands of a trained and experienced gunner, the weapons would behave completely differently one day to how they did the next. The problem was the gunpowder.

Gunpowder in the 15th century was a simple mix of charcoal, sulphur and saltpetre for as yet no way had been found of combining the three into a stable powder. Such powder was unpredictable, would not explode when damp and rarely performed as expected. Guns, therefore, tended to be viewed as potentially useful battlefield weapons, but not as reliable as arrows or swords.

For centuries the battlefield had been ruled by the armoured knight on horseback. A well timed charge by heavy horsemen had been able to smash enemy formations and win a battle with ease. From 1346 onwards, however, the English had rendered this tactic obsolete with a novel tactical formation. The English put their armoured men on foot, drawn up in a line between four and eight ranks deep. The men stood shoulder to shoulder to form a solid block of men. A high proportion of these men were armed with pole weapons of one sort or another. At first these were mostly spears, but by the time of the Wars of the Roses these had mostly been replaced by bills. Horses will not run headlong into a solid barrier, be it a brick wall or a mass of men. So long as the men on foot stood their ground, charging cavalry would come to a halt. The horsemen would then be vulnerable to the pole weapons of the infantry.

Standing on the flanks of the densely packed armoured infantry were bodies of archers. What made archery so effective was the fact that the archers were using a tactic that became known as the arrowstorm. Instead of the archers being dispersed among the arrayed infantry they were grouped together as solid groups

Most armoured infantry during the Wars of the Roses were armed something like this figure. He wears an iron helmet and full upper harness composed of breastplate with groin plates over a mail shirt. His lower arms and hands are protected by plate armour gauntlets. His legs are quite unprotected. His main weapon is a bill, a weapon on a shaft over six feet long that combined a thrusting point with a chopping blade and sometimes, as here, a back hook to pull enemies to the ground. He has a sword to use in case his bill breaks or for close infighting.

of archers. This enabled them for the first time to come under the command of an experienced knight whose sole task was to direct the archery. A group of archers could be ordered to shoot at the same time at the same target.

By the Wars of the Roses this arrowstorm had become slightly less decisive. Knights usually fought on foot and new types of armour had been invented. This new armour took the form of steel plates shaped to wrap around the body. The plate armour was also designed to have smooth shapes and flowing profiles so that an arrow would glance off it more easily.

Nevertheless the usual battlefield tactic at this date was still to deploy knights and men at arms in a solid phalanx, flanked by archers. Sometimes groups of archers were put at intervals along the line of armoured men. While the archers were effective at a distance, they were vulnerable to armoured infantry at close quarters and so they might fall back behind the men at arms when the enemy closed to hand to hand fighting. More heavily armoured archers, as was increasingly common by the later 15th century, would join the hand to hand fighting.

Although heavily armoured, mounted knights had fallen out of use there was still a role for horsemen. As noted above, Irish horsemen were sometimes hired to serve as scouts, but most commanders preferred to use Englishmen equipped as hobilars. These hobilars - also known as currours or prickers - were more lightly armed than knights and rode less expensive horses. Their roles were mostly off the battlefield. They scouted ahead and to the flanks of the army looking for the enemy. They rode ahead to secure bridges or fords. They rode off to carry

This fully armoured knight wears the very latest and finest armour, so he must be a rich man. The body is entirely encased in plates of quality steel shaped to fit the individual. Pieces of mail are used to give added protection at joints. His main weapon is a poleaxe, with a long sword as a secondary weapon. This sort of armour was surprisingly light and flexible, allowing the wearer freedom of movement.

A standard infantry formation from the Wars of the Roses. The armoured billmen and men at arms are formed up four ranks deep in the centre while the archers are pushed forward on the flanks to shoot at the advancing enemy. The commanding knight and his assistants stand behind to direct movement.

messages to other commanders or to local authorities. They sought good campsites, bought - or in France stole - food supplies.

Even on the field of battle these hobilars had a use. They were kept in reserve to be unleashed on a fleeing enemy to use their speed to ride down fugitives. Or they could be thrown into action to disrupt a pursuit by enemy horsemen and so cover the retreat of the infantry.

In the context of the Wars of the Roses, armies tended to be commanded by the most politically important nobleman present. It tended to be these men who had called the army into existence and who decided what its purpose was to be. There were usually Constables present, and here their role seems to have been to offer advice when asked for it. They might be asked their opinion on any matter, but it was always up the nobleman in charge what decision to make. It was, in a very real sense, his head that was going to be on the block if anything went wrong.

19

Chapter 4
The Battle of Towton
The First Day

E dward IV had ordered his various commanders to meet him at Pontefract by 27 March. He arrived on that day, having marched from London by way of Cambridge. The size of the army that gathered in Pontefract has been the subject of a great deal of controversy. Since the size of the armies involved has relevance both to the conduct of the fighting and to the scene of the battle it is worth having a look at the issue.

The main source for the size and composition of Edward's army is a history written by a London merchant named Edward Hall. The book was first published in 1542, some 80 years after the Battle of Towton. Although this is rather late, we know that Hall went to considerable lengths to get hold of accurate information and to compare different versions of the same event. Whenever his work can be checked it turns out to be accurate. According to Hall, Edward had a total of 48,640 men gathered in Pontefract. Hall says that he got this information from the paybook of Edward's chief accountant.

This is a huge number, and most modern historians doubt that it is accurate. They point out that most contemporary armies were less than half that size, and that commanders had considerable practical difficulties handling bodies of men over 20,000 strong. These difficulties had much to do with the practical business of marching so many men along the narrow roads of the time, finding somewhere for them all to camp in one place with adequate access to drinking water and firewood. Modern historians also point out the difficulties of mustering men for war at this period and the issues of paying them, feeding them and gathering them together. Figures of ranging between 10,000 and 25,000 have been suggested for Edward's army at Pontefract.

However, there is no real reason why Hall should be disbelieved. We know from other sources that Edward had gone to considerable efforts to gather as many

The Towton Campaign began as Edward IV arrived at Pontefract on his way to York, where his Lancastrian enemies were based. The first day of fighting saw Edward force his way over the flooded River Aire at Ferrybridge and Castleford, though not before the Lancastrians had scored an early success and nearly casued the Yorkist army to break up in panic and confusion. Not for the first time Edward's level head and leadership saved the day.

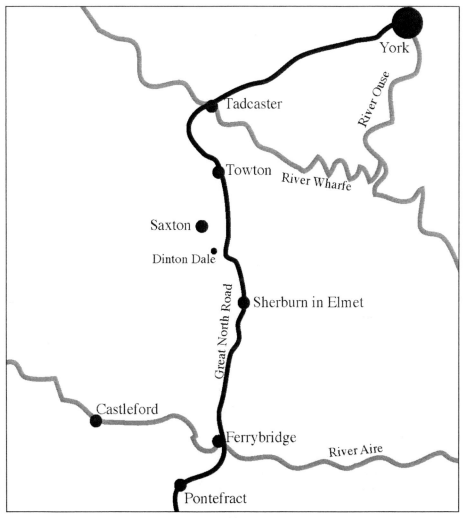

Bridge Street in Pontefract. King Edward IV was staying in a house in the town centre while his army was camped outside.

men as possible, and that the merchants of London had donated huge sums of money to enable him to do so. He had also marched north at a leisurely rate specifically to enable a large army to gather. That army had come to Pontefract by various routes and divided into several smaller armies, which would have made the task of moving and feeding them easier. As we will see, Edward did encounter problems moving his combined army, indicating that it was very large.

Moreover, every contemporary writer states that the army Edward had at Pontefract was the largest army the Yorkists ever fielded. and it is worth noting that Hall states his total of 48,640 being the number of men in Pontefract, not that they were all soldiers. Any army of this date would have had certainly 15% and perhaps up to 25% of its number made up of squires, pages, cooks, armourers and other non-combatants.

Assuming Hall's figure to be correct Edward may have had 36,000 fighting men in Pontefract on 27 March. This was an impressively vast army, but Edward had good intelligence that indicated that the Lancastrian army was even bigger. We have no even remotely reliable figures for the size of the Lancastrian host, although all contemporaries agree that it was larger than the Yorkist army. It is beyond doubt, therefore, that the Battle of Towton was in terms of numbers of men involved the greatest battle ever fought in Britain.

The Lancastrians were in York on the day Edward arrived in Pontefract. Between the two armies lay the River Wharfe and River Aire. Both rivers flow west to east to fall into the Ouse, which flows north to York, and both rivers were in flood after heavy rain and with melting snows from the hills and moors to the west. Neither river could be forded by an army on the march with its baggage, artillery and camp followers, and the Lancastrians had broken down all the bridges.

Edward's first move was, therefore, to gain control of a bridge and repair it. He chose the most obvious bridge, that at Ferrybridge where the Great North Road crossed the Aire. The old wooden bridge built in 1198 had been replaced with one of stone in the 1390s, and it seems that the Lancastrians had broken down one arch of this structure.

Edward sent forward the Earl of Warwick, commander of the Vanguard, to take Ferrybridge and repair the bridge. Warwick moved with his customary speed and skill. By late afternoon he had control of the crossing and his men were busily bridging the broken arch with a temporary timber structure. Warwick sent a small body of men under Lord Fitzwalter to the north bank of the Aire to watch the road coming south from York and stop any effort by the Lancastrians to stop work on the bridge. With Lord Fitzwalter was Thomas Neville, Warwick's illegitimate half brother.

Meanwhile the Lancastrian high command, such as it was, had been discussing the situation. Learning that Edward was just south of the Aire with a smaller army than themselves, the Lancastrians decided to advance. It is unclear if King Henry VI marched with the army or not, though later events would indicate he did not. It would seem that Queen Margaret and young Prince Edward stayed with him. The Lancastrian army therefore marched south under the command of three men: The Duke of Somerset, the Earl of Northumberland and John, Baron Clifford. Of the three Somerset may have been the overall leader, but it is difficult to be certain.

What is known is that Baron Clifford was in charge of the hobilars, those lightly armed horsemen who rode ahead of an army to scout for the enemy, find camping

The bridge at Ferrybridge today was built about 400 years after the battle but it stands on almost the exact site of the medieval bridge that crossed the River Aire in 1461.

grounds and check the condition of the roads. After exchanging words with Northumberland about which of them was the braver, Clifford decided to prove his worth by making an attack on the Yorkists at Ferrybridge.

At the same time the Earl of Northumberland set off for Castleford. His intention seems to have been to block the ford and deny its use to Edward. However he had further to go, and had a mixed force of infantry and cavalry that moved more slowly than did the hobilars of Clifford.

At some point in the early hours of the morning, while it was still dark, the Lancastrian horsemen charged into the camp on the north bank of the Aire. Lord Fitzwalter was asleep in a bed in a nearby cottage. Hearing the commotion he thought that some of his more quarrelsome men had started a brawl. He leapt out of bed, grabbed a poleaxe and ran out in his nightshirt to sort out the dispute. He was cut down almost immediately by a Lancastrian horseman, his lack of armour making him an easy victim.

Thomas Neville, widely known as the Bastard of Salisbury, was also killed although nobody saw him go down amid the mayhem and confusion of the night raid. The Yorkists were taken completely by surprise and those who did not flee promptly were killed by Clifford and his men.

As the sounds of battle were heard on the south bank of the river, Warwick hastily donned his armour, grabbed his sword and mustered his men for battle. They evidently could not see much of what was going on, it was after all still night, but soon flames shot up as the Lancastrians put the camp to the torch. Then Clifford led some of his men on to the north end of the broken bridge. His intention seems to have been to stop any Yorkist reinforcements from crossing the Aire, and to see if he could smash down whatever repairs had been begun.

Warwick saw the Lancastrians moving forward and seems to have panicked. Hall said he was "like a man made desperate". He leapt on to his riding horse, not bothering to find his war horse, and galloped off to Pontefract. Warwick galloped into Pontefract an hour or so before dawn, bringing with him as many men of his as had managed to find a horse. The flight from Ferrybridge had all the hallmarks of a rout and of panic. Warwick was not normally someone to panic, so his sudden arrival would have been all the more dramatic.

Edward was woken by his guards and told that horsemen were demanding entrance to Pontefract. Learning it was Warwick who wanted access into the town, he threw on some clothes and ordered the gates to be opened. He sent men running to fetch Fauconberg, then went out into the street to meet Warwick. It was to be a dramatic meeting.

Warwick pulled his rushing horse to a halt in the street and sat gasping for air in front of Edward. "Sire," gasped Warwick, "I pray that God have mercy on their souls - those who in the beginning of your enterprise have lost their lives. And because I see no chance of help in this World, I leave it to God our creator and redeemer to take vengeance for their lives and bring justice on their slayers." Warwick then leapt down from his horse as his men milled around in the street.

Realising that the scene around him was one of confusion and perhaps despair, Warwick leapt to the conclusion that many of the army were preparing to flee. He dramatically whipped out his sword and slit the throat of his horse so that it fell dead on the cobbles.

"Let him fly who will fly," shouted Warwick. "For surely I will tarry with him that will tarry with me." He then knelt down in front of the bewildered Edward and kissed the hilt of his sword before bowing his head.

As this dramatic scene was ending Fauconberg arrived. Together with Edward they dragged Warwick to one side and managed to find out what had happened at Ferrybridge. It seems that Warwick was incapable of giving a clear picture of what had happened. Clearly the outpost on the north bank had been overrun, but beyond that all was confusion. Edward sent scouts riding out to find out what was happening just four miles to the northeast.

Meanwhile, news of Warwick's sudden arrival and dramatic horse-slaying was spreading like wildfire through the Yorkist army. Warwick had already fought at 7 battles in the previous six years, performing valiantly in them all. That he had fled a Lancastrian attack did not bode well, nor did his declaration that he did not

The site of the old ford at Castleford is now covered by this dramatically modern footbridge. The modern road bridge is a short distance downstream.

expect anyone to be able to avenge the deaths of those who had died. His subsequent gesture of killing his horse smacked of panic not of calm consideration. Disquiet spread through the camp, men woke up to learn the bad news and wondered what it meant.

Edward was quick to notice what was going on. Medieval battles depended very much on the morale of the men, and Edward was in no mood to take any chances. He hurriedly scribbled out a proclamation and ordered his officers to read it aloud to their units. It cleverly played on the pride and greed of the men under his commanded.

"I give my permission," it ran, "to any man who is afraid to fight alongside me to depart at once. Be gone. But those who will tarry with me here and give battle will be given great payment. And with this addition: Any soldier who should voluntarily abide but who then in, or before, the conflict to come should fly or turn his back to the enemy - he I will kill. And any who should kill such a man will have double his wages from my hands."

As the officers passed through the army reading out this proclamation, Edward ordered Fauconberg to take a force of Yorkish horsemen to Ferrybridge. They were not to ride directly to the south side of the river, but were to first head eight miles west to Castleford and cross the swollen river by the ford there. Fauconberg left at dawn, taking with him Sir Walter Blount and Sir Robert Horne and their men.

As Fauconberg rode off, Edward gave the orders for his entire army to eat breakfast and to get into marching order. The rearguard under the Earl of Norfolk was to march to Ferrybridge along with the baggage and artillery. Once there, Norfolk was to repair the bridge, then cross and head for Tadcaster taking the Great North Road through Sherburn in Elmet. Edward himself was to take the vanguard and main body of the army and follow Fauconberg to cross the Aire at Castleford before heading northeast to join the Great North Road at Sherbun in Elmet himself.

It would seem from these orders that Edward believed that the Lancastrian force that had raided Ferrybridge had been merely a raiding party of hobilars. He must have thought that main Lancastrian army was still in York, or at least on the far side of the Wharfe. If so, he was in for a nasty shock.

The first sign that Edward had that things were not going as he expected came when Fauconberg reported back that he had found Lancastrian scouts at Castleford. When these men were challenged they had not ridden east towards

Ferrybridge, as they would have done if they were part of Clifford's force, but north. The scouts were, in fact, part of Northumberland's force. Northumberland had not reached the Aire at Castleford by dawn as he had intended and was still some distance to the north. Nothing more is heard of Northumberland on the 28th, so it is assumed that having failed to block the ford he turned around and marched back to rejoin Somerset and the main Lancastrian army.

Fauconberg, meanwhile, was now heading east along the north bank of the Aire hoping to catch Clifford at Ferrybridge as Norfolk came up from the south. It was not to be. Clifford seems to have had his own scouts out and was warned in plenty of time. He did as much damage to the Yorkist repair work at the bridge as he could, then turned and rode north the way he had come up the Great North Road. He and his men went north through Byram, South Milford, Sherburn in Elmet and Barkstone Ash. He then ordered his men to dismount and take a break in a little valley called Dinting Dale.

As the Lancastrian horsemen dismounted, to eat food from their pouches and slake their thirsts, Baron Clifford decided to attend to something that had been bothering him since early that morning. His gorget had been chafing his skin. The gorget was the piece of armour that was attached to the breastplate and which rose up to cover the neck, throat and chin while the helmet came down to overlap the gorget from above. Clifford took off his helmet, then asked a companion to undo the small clips holding his gorget in place. The armour was removed and Clifford began fiddling with it to try to ease the rubbing that was irritating him.

It was at this moment that an arrow struck Clifford in the throat, sending him falling to the ground with blood pumping from the wound. The arrow was just the first of a great shower of deadly arrows that plunged down into the Lancastrian horsemen. The arrows were followed by a charge of horsemen, who swept down into Dinting Dale screaming their war cries. Clifford was not the only nobleman to die, John Neville, the Baron Neville and brother of the Earl of Westmoreland, was also cut down. The majority of the Lancastrians were killed before they could mount up and ride off, though some got away to carry the news of what had happened to the Duke of Somerset.

Somerset had meanwhile spent the day getting the main Lancastrian army over the Wharfe at Tadcaster, but due to the time it took to get his huge army over the narrow bridge he decided to camp just outside the town. He chose an area south of the town where the small River Cock flowed into the Wharfe from the south. News of the movements of Northumberland and Clifford reached him in the afternoon. It is likely that Somerset rode south from Tadcaster that afternoon to spy out the land. Certainly he knew by nightfall exactly what he was going to do next day. He gave orders that the army was to be up before dawn, was to eat breakfast and arm itself for battle. It would then head south down the Great North Road toward the Yorkists.

Edward, meanwhile, seems to have still been ignorant that the main enemy army was so close. He camped his main army somewhere near Sherburn in Elmet, though it is not known quite where. He knew that enemy outposts and scouts were nearby, but seems to have expected that the next day would be spent quietly marching the 8 miles to Tadcaster, where he might have to fight his way over the Wharfe.

Blissfully unaware that the Duke of Somerset was at that moment plotting his death and destruction, Edward fell asleep soon after dusk on 27th March.

The Oddfellow's Arms in Sherburn in Elmet. The Yorkist army camped in the fields outside this village the night before the battle.

Chapter 5
The Battle of Towton - Second Day

The Lancastrian army was up early on Sunday 29 March 1461. Well before dawn the lead units were breaking camp and marching south along the Great North Road. In late March dawn comes over Yorkshire a little before 6am. On 29 March 1461 the dawn came cold and grey. Heavy clouds covered the sky and a bitterly cold east wind lashed the landscape. It must have been an uncomfortable night for the men camped out, and they rose cold and chilled. If they had a hot breakfast it will have been welcome, and the march south may have warmed them but the day remained cold and windy. Those left behind in the camp packed away the equipment and prepared to march. They needed only to await the news of the coming battle to know which way to go.

Somerset led his men south, but as they passed through the village of Towton the Lancastrians veered to their right and left the road to climb up on to a hill which rose 100 feet above the Plain of York. This hill, or plateau, has a flat top that runs 2 miles north to south and about three quarters of a mile east to west. About two thirds of the way from the north the plateau is divided in two by a shallow valley about 30 feet deep that is known as Towton Dale. The plateau to the north of Towton Dale is known as Renshaw Hill, the part to the south as Castle Hill (though there does not seem to have ever been a castle here).

The position occupied by the Lancastrian army was on the southern end of Renshaw Hill facing down into Towton Dale. This was a strong defensive position. On the right of the line the slopes of Renshaw Hill fell steeply down to the River Cock. Many people might at first glance take the Cock to be more a narrow stream than a river, but appearances can be deceptive for the waters can be deep and Hall says that on the day of the battle were over 4 feet deep. The front of the position faced down the slope into Towton Dale. While these slopes are not especially steep they do fall over 30 feet to the foot of the dale. Any army launching an attack would have to first go down the opposite slope from Castle Hill, then climb up Renshaw Hill. The eastern slopes of Renshaw were also fairly shallow, but they fell a hundred feet down to the road from Ferrybridge to Tadcaster. The flat lands east of the road were boggy and marshy - today they are covered by a golf course that is kept dry by numerous drainage ditches, but they were not there in 1461.

Somerset had therefore chosen well. His right flank was protected by a deep river and steep slopes, while his left was covered by marshy ground that no armoured man could get across. His front was, for the most part protected by a slope and only on the extreme left did it face an attack across flat ground.

It is not entirely clear from the account written by the chronicler Hall exactly how Somerset deployed his men. It would seem, however, that the Earl of Northumberland had command of the vanguard and was on the right of the Lancastrian line. Next to Northumberland was Sir Andrew Trollope, who presumably therefore commanded the centre.

Somerset's position is unknown. He may have commanded the left wing which, being on flat ground might be the most vulnerable. On the other hand he may have held a reserve under his own command behind the main line. There is certainly a slight rise in the ground about where the current battle monument stands that although slight would have been enough to give Somerset a view over the heads of the men in front of him. Somerset also had enough men to allow him to have a separate reserve. The position between the slopes dropping to the Cock and the marshes is about 1,100 yards, so he had around 35 men to the yard.

We do know that Somerset detached one group of men, apparently around 9,000. These men were sent forward to form up in a long line along the crest of Castle Hill facing south. From there they could see - and be seen from - the road heading south to Sherburn in Elmet and Ferrybridge. It seems that this forward detachment of the Lancastrians was in place by 8am. Presumably the rest of the vast army was at this point still marching south from Tadcaster and taking up its position.

The Yorkist army had, meanwhile, been in no hurry to get moving. It was less than three hours march to Tadcaster, where Edward was expecting to face another contested river crossing. With 12 hours of daylight there must have seemed to be plenty of time. It was around 8am that the vanguard got going north under Fauconberg. At 9am Fauconberg heard a great shout go up from his forward troops. Spurring his horse forward Fauconberg came over the shoulder of Windmill Hill. As he did so he saw the 9,000 men that Somerset had posted on the southern crest of Castle Hill.

Realising that this was no scouting party and that the main Lancastrian army might be nearby, Fauconburg sent a messenger galloping south to alert Edward, who was still in camp at Sherburn in Elmet. As soon as he got the message, Edward raced up to the top of the church tower, but the bulk of Windmill Hill blocked his view of the Lancastrians. All he could see was the long sinuous column of his own army strung out on the road marching north. He climbed back down, armed himself for battle and rode north to join Fauconberg.

As he joined Fauconberg on Windmill Hill, Edward had to decide what to do, and it was not an easy decision to make. Edward did not have his entire army with him. Norfolk and the rearguard were still back at Ferrybridge repairing the

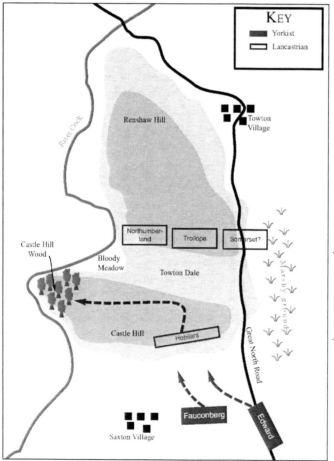

The second day of battle began as the Yorkist army was marching north along the Great North Road. They were not expecting to meet anything more than a small force guarding the bridge over the Cock north of Towton and so were surprised to see a force of hobilar cavalry on the crest of Castle Hill. The hobilars fell back, luring the Yorkists into advancing close to the main Lancastrian army.

bridge so that the artillery, baggage and supply carts could be got over the swollen River Aire. Edward knew that the Lancastrian army was larger than his own. The cautious thing to do would be to wait until Norfolk and his men got over the river and came up to join Edward. But it was likely to be a long wait. The bridge would take hours to mend, then the carts and artillery would take hours more to get over it. Norfolk was unlikely to approach that day.

On the other hand, the Lancastrians on Castle Hill numbered only about 9,000 or so. Edward had enough men with him to outnumber them by at least two to one, maybe more. Dealing with a large part of the enemy's army before the main force came up was a tempting opportunity.

Edward decided to attack. He sent orders back to Norfolk telling him not to wait for the transport and artillery. As soon as the bridge was passable he was to cross over with his fighting men and hurry north as fast as possible. Edward then issued a proclamation to be read out by the officers to their men. Edward ordered that no prisoners were to be taken and no wounded enemy saved, everyone was to be killed. This will have come as a disappointment to the Yorkist men. This was not so much out of feelings of pity or mercy, but because holding prisoners for ransom was a recognised and respectable way to make money in medieval warfare. Indeed a man who managed to capture a nobleman could be set up for life, earning easily enough money to buy a farm or tavern, which would provide him with a comfortable income. Perhaps to make up for this disappointment, Edward promised to pay a reward for the heads of certain specified Lancastrian nobles. Sir Andrew Trollope's head, for instance, was worth £100 - the equivalent of 22 years pay to the average labourer.

As soon as Edward and Fauconberg had their men formed up they began the march north up the slopes of Castle Hill. Again, it is impossible to know exactly what formation the Yorkists adopted but we do know that Fauconberg faced Northumberland, so if Northumberland was on the Lancastrian right wing then Fauconburg must have been on the Yorkist left. That leaves Edward to be on the right. Norfolk and the rearguard were absent, but a conventional position would have put them on the right so this formation does make sense.

As soon as the Yorkists moved the Lancastrians on Castle Hill wheeled around and disappeared over the crest of the hill, heading north.

Edward and Fauconberg led their men up the slope to the southern crest of the plateau. The flat land in front of them seemed to be empty. There was no sign of the Lancastrians. Advancing another 200 yards brought the Yorkists to the summit of Castle Hill, and now they could see the Lancastrians. There were not 9,000 men facing them but the entire strength of the enemy army - or so it seemed.

In fact Somerset had laid a trap for the Yorkists. Not only had he successfully lured them into battle, he had also ordered the 9,000 men he had sent forward not to fall back to join the main army but to head west and hide in the extensive woods that covered the western end of Castle Hill. There they were to lie down in silence and await an opportunity to launch a devastating surprise assault on the flank of the Yorkists.

Somerset had got Edward exactly where he wanted him. But that is when things began to go horribly wrong for the Lancastrians.

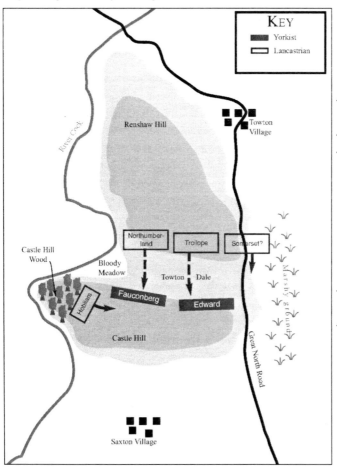

Having been lured forwards, Edward and Fauconberg found themselves faced by the main Lancastrian army while their own rearguard under the Earl of Norfolk was still several miles to the south. Even worse, an ambush force of hobilars was hidden on their flank in Castle Hill Wood. The battle began in a snowstorm, which may have served to confuse the combatants as to the true layout of the battle.

It was the weather that first took a hand. The bitterly cold wind that had been blowing steadily from the east suddenly moved round to the south, though it remained just as chill. Moments later a heavy deluge of snow fell from the skies, Hall calls it a "snyt of snow". The combination of heavy snow and driving wind gave the wily and experienced Fauconberg the chance he was looking for.

Fauconberg ordered his archers to hurry forward from the Yorkist lines. He then had them shoot a couple of shots only of arrows. He also told his men to use their special "flight arrows", that is long-range arrows fitted with extra feathers and of a lighter construction. These arrows fell among the Lancastrian army, who not unnaturally shot back. Fauconberg had meanwhile pulled his own men back again. Shooting into the snow the Lancastrians could not see the fall of their shot very well and were unaware of the fact that the wind was causing their arrows to fall short of the Yorkists. Hall says the Lancastrian arrows fell "9 tailor's yards" short of the Yorkist line.

When the Lancastrians had used up all their arrows, Fauconberg sent his men forwards again. This time they began pulling the Lancastrian arrows out of the ground and shooting them at the enemy. This time they shot in earnest, not just one or two shots, and began inflicting serious casualties on the men facing them. The hapless Northumberland was caught without arrows with which to reply to the Yorkist fusillade.

The Lancastrian plan had been to wait on Renshaw Hill for Yorkists to exhaust themselves in a futile uphill attack, but now Northumberland's men were dying and he was helpless to do anything to protect them. Apparently on his own initiative Northumberland decided to attack. He led his men down the slope from Renshaw Hill into Towton Dale, then up the far side of the shallow valley to climb Castle Hill. As his men approached the Yorkist army they started walking through the arrows that they had shot earlier and many of which still stuck up from the ground. Several Lancastrians tripped and fell, disrupting the formation as it moved to close with the Yorkists.

Fauconberg had by this point pulled his archers back to his main formation and was awaiting the attack of Northumberland's men. The Lancastrian formation was badly disrupted and weakened by arrow casualties, but it still outnumbered the Yorkists.

Meanwhile others in the Lancastrian army had seen Northumberland's men advancing. The snowstorm seems to have ceased as Northumberland reached the bottom of Towton Dale. Trollope in the Lancastrian centre must have wondered

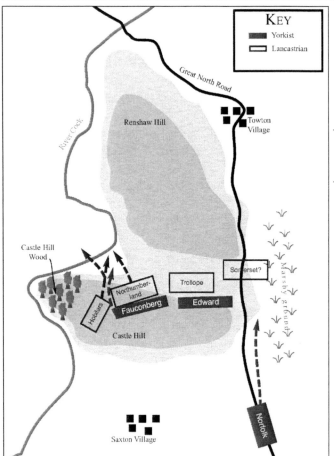

KEY
■ Yorkist
□ Lancastrian

Great North Road

Renshaw Hill

River Cock

Towton Village

Castle Hill Wood

Hobilars

Northumberland

Fauconberg

Trollope

Edward

Somerset?

Castle Hill

Marshy ground

Saxton Village

Norfolk

The battle began to go wrong for the Lancastrians when their attack on the left flank of the Yorkist army was first halted and then pushed back down the steep hill into a flat area on the banks of the River Cock. The Lancastrians were trapped against the river and slaughtered by the victorious Yorkists. At about the same time Norfolk's men appeared on the scene, marching up the Great North Road in a massive column.

what Northumberland was up to, but knew that he had to support his comrade or he might see Northumberland's men surrounded and slaughtered. So down the slope when Trollope and the centre, though he moved later and perhaps with less determination than did Northumberland.

The Lancastrian left wing does not seem to have advanced at first, perhaps if Somerset had personal command here he may have wanted to stick to the original plan, or perhaps it was the lie of the land that caused the hesitation. It is possible that the Lancastrian left wing was blocking the road and so was down on the lower ground and eastern slopes of Renshaw Hill. If Edward had his right flank on the top of Castle Hill then whoever commanded the Lancastrian left wing would have been faced by a long 100 foot high climb to get up to Edward.

Meanwhile, events were moving fast on the Yorkist left wing. As Northumberland's men clashed with Fauconberg's the murderous hand to hand fighting that was such a key feature of medieval battles got under way. The men may have been trained to fight wearing full armour, but it was still an exhausting business to wield swords, axes and polearms. The nervous energy needed to stare death in the face, hacking at enemies standing no more than two feet away while they sought to crush your skull or slash your body to pieces was tremendous. Few men could manage it for long, so there was a constant shifting as men jostled for position, stepped back and others came forward to get at the enemy. Men engaged in the front line did not dare take their eyes off the enemy to their front for that was the way to a quick and a gory death. Understandably most men looked forwards in battle, watching for a chance to strike or for an enemy blow to avoid.

And so when the Lancastrians lurking in Castle Hill Woods emerged to seize their chance the Yorkists did not at first see them.

The only source we have for what happened next is the Burgundian chronicler Jehan de Waurin. He wrote his History of England in 1467 and claims to have spoken to many men who lived in England, or at least visited the kingdom. He says that the surprise Lancastrian attack was led by "mounted spearmen". Presumably he means hobilars, but we cannot be certain.

However it was composed, the Lancastrian ambush party came surging out of the woodland and charged toward Fauconberg's men. The Yorkists saw the danger just in time to form a defensive line, but it was a close thing. Fauconberg's men were being pushed back when Edward himself appeared on the scene. Perhaps he brought fresh men with him, but certainly he enthused his men with the sort of personal courage and leadership that medieval commanders had to show. "Edward so courageously comforted his men, refreshed the weary and helping the wounded," says Hall, "that the enemy were dicomfited and overcome."

It was at this point that a disaster overwhelmed the Lancastrian right wing.

The struggle around Fauconberg's left wing launched by the Lancastrian ambush had been fought out on the northwestern corner of Castle Hill. At this point the River Cock curved in a meander that cut deep into the high ground at the point where the Towton Dale dropped down to the river. The slopes here were very steep and fell a hundred feet down to meadows flanking the Cock.

Edward's new attack pushed the Lancastrians over the edge of this slope, sending them slithering down to the treacherous marshy meadows far below. The jubilant Yorkists gave chase, hacking and slashing at the fleeing men with enthusiasm. The massacre that followed was horrific. The Lancastrians could not get away for they were hemmed in by the Cock to the west, the sheer slope of Renshaw Hill to the north and the vengeful Yorkists to the south. Some fugitives tried to get over the river, but found the water deeper than they expected. They lost their footing and drowned, pushed down by the mob that followed. Those who got stuck in the mud of the marsh were butchered, those that reached the river drowned, those that turned to fight were slaughtered. In places the Cock was blocked by the bodies of the dead and dying, tempting fugitives to run over the bodies only to be shot down by Yorkist archers or to slip to their doom. So many Lancastrians were killed in this comparatively small area of ground that it was possible to walk from the foot of Castle Hill to the River Cock by stepping only on the dead. The place has been called "Bloody Meadow" ever since.

Three miles to the north a cook's boy cleaning pots at the Lancastrian camp at Tadcaster gave a sudden cry. A dead body was floating past in the River Cock. Others came to watch as other bodies came past. Then the water turned a dark,

The Bloody Meadow looking north toward the original Lancastrian position. The Cock Stream is to the left and the Yorkist position is to the right. It was this patch of land that saw the bitterest fighting of the battle.

ominous red as the blood of the dead came downstream so thickly that the water itself turned red. The men and camp followers gathered on the banks of the Cock to gaze in awe and trepidation at the horrible flow. They must have wondered what it meant.

Back at the battle the slaughter of the Lancastrian right wing was coming to an end. Despite the carnage the Lancastrians still outnumbered the Yorkists, but that was about to change. It would seem to have been soon after noon that a column of men came marching north over the eastern shoulder of Windmill Hill up the road from Ferrybridge. The banners and flags that floated over the mass of armed men showed that this was the Yorkist rearguard commanded by the Duke of Norfolk. According to Hall, Norfolk had been taken ill and the division was being marched into action under the command of Sir John Wenlock and Sir John Dynham.

Whoever led the rearguard, paused as they came up on to the right flank of the Yorkist army. The men were deployed into battle formation and then launched

A Victorian view of the horrific scenes as the Yorkists with the weight of numbers and the slope behind them drove the Lancaastrian right wing into the waters of the River Cock to drown or be hacked to death.

forward to attack the left wing of the Lancastrian army, which had already shown itself to be less committed to the attack than the right and centre. Whoever commanded the Lancastrian left proved unable to provide the kind of inspired leadership that Edward had given on the Yorkist left. The Lancastrian left wing began to crumble as small groups of men began to break away and flee north.

The disintegration of the Lancastrian force gathered pace as the long day started to come to an end. An early dusk settled in as the heavily clouded sky blocked the weak evening sun. As darkness fell the Lancastrian centre gave way and fell back.

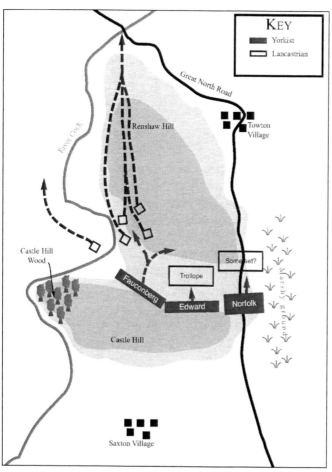

As the Lancasatrian right wing collapsed into a mass of fleeing fugitives, Faucunberg sought to move his men round to attack the flank of the men commanded by Trollope. Some Yorkists could not resist the temptation to pursue the fleeing Lancastrians, cut them down and rob their bodies, but most followed their banners and put intolerable pressure on to Trollope just as Norfolk's men smashed into the Lancastrian left wing.

At this point a Yorkist soldier armed with a crossbow spotted among the retreating Lancastrians the Lord Dacre who had killed his father at an earlier battle. The soldier scrambled into the branches of what was recorded at the time as a "bur tree", an elder, to get a better shot. The bolt was loosed and at an impressively great range of 300 yards Lord Dacre fell dead. Even at the time the shot was recognised as having been a remarkable one and the elder tree became famous.

What followed was not an orderly retreat, but nor was it a total rout. In places Lancastrian units fell apart and the men were cut down by the pursuing Yorkist hobilars. But other retreating units kept their formation well and fought off any effort to intercept them. There was something of a bottleneck where the road to

Dacre's Cross stands close to the spot where Lord Dacre's body was found after the battle. Dacre is generally thought to have been killed just behind the centre of the Lancastrian line as the collapse of the Lancastrian force gathered pace. The cross to be seen today has been restored more than once and there is some evidence that it has been moved from its original position. It now stands beside the B1217 just under a mile south of Towton village.

Tadcaster crossed the River Cock, and bloodshed here was particularly savage.

"The chase continued all night," recorded Hall, "and the most part of the next day and every time they [the Lancastrians] perceived any advantage they returned to the battle again and fought with their enemies to the great loss of them all."

The chase went on for many hours, with some Lancastrian fugitives being pursued all the way to the gates of York. The eventual death toll was enormous and effectively settled the dispute between York and Lancaster for a generation.

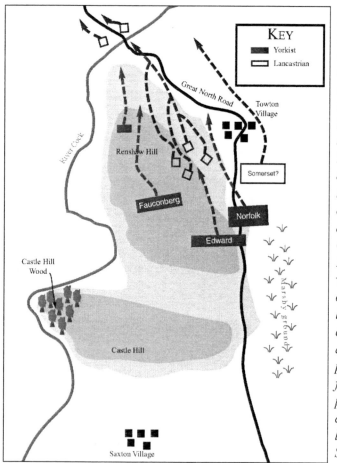

KEY

■ Yorkist
□ Lancastrian

In the final stages of the battle the Lancastrian right and centre fled in disorder. Their commanders, Northumberland and Trollope, were killed in this stage of the battle, hastening the collapse of order among their men. Other parts of the Lancastrian army withdrew in good order and even launched counterattacks agatinst the pursuing Yorkists, a feat that can probably be put down to the leadership of Somerset.

Chapter 6
Aftermath

The immediate aftermath of the Battle of Towton consisted of clearing up the dead bodies. There were a great many of them. The heralds had the task of identifying the bodies of any knights and noblemen so that their next of kin could be informed and arrangements made for their burial.

Clifford, Neville and Dacre had been killed early, while the Earl of Northumberland and Sir Andrew Trollope were killed later in the battle. Their bodies were collected up and taken away for burial. Northumberland was taken to York where he was buried in St Denys Church, Walmgate. His tomb was destroyed when half the church collapsed in 1797 due to bungled building works next door. Lord Dacre's body was taken to Saxton, just south of the battlefield, and buried in the grave yard of All Saints Church. His family took the unusual step of burying him upright mounted on his warhorse, which had also been killed in the battle. His tomb remains, though it is much weathered.

The bodies of the commoners did not receive careful treatment. Great pits were dug and the bodies tipped in, though a decent Christian burial service was performed for them. One grave pit is known to have been dug in Bloody Meadow, and another was behind the Yorkist left wing on the way to Saxton. Two more were between the centre of the Lancastrian line and Towton village. The larger of these grave pits was recorded at the time to be 19 yards wide and 32 yards long, though its depth is unknown.

The total number of men killed at Towton is as controversial as the numbers of men who fought there. The heralds who identified the nobles and the knights, and who supervised the mass burials, reported to Edward a few days later that they had buried 28,000 bodies in all. The heralds were including those killed at Ferrybridge, at Dinting Dale and during the long pursuit after the battle as well as at the battle itself.

This figure is given in two separate documents, the first a letter written by a Yorkist knight to his family back home and the second a letter written by Edward himself to his mother. It seems reasonable to conclude, therefore, that the figure of 28,000 was the one given by the heralds to Edward. Since the heralds and Edward were all there, they should know. Other contemporary documents, written by men who were not present, seem to repeat the heralds' figures when they record that "nearly 30,000" or "about 30,000" men died. This death toll would make Towton far and away the bloodiest battle ever fought in Britain.

The day after the battle, Edward IV and his army rode into York through Micklegate Bar. He ordered that the severed heads of his father and brother be taken down from spikes over the gate and buried with their bodies, but did not exact revenge on the people of York. Edward generally preferred to win people to his side rather than to take bloody vengeance.

The day after the battle Edward crossed the River Wharfe unopposed and rode into the city of York. The mayor and officials of the city met him with bowed heads and great solemnity. They professed their loyalty to him, as they had done to King Henry VI only a few days earlier, and paid a hefty "voluntary donation" by way of proving their loyalty. Edward pocketed the cash and exacted no reprisals on the city. Instead he ordered that the heads of his father, brother and uncle be taken down from the spikes over the city gates and buried alongside their bodies in Pontefract Priory. Once Edward was secure on his throne he had the bodies exhumed and reinterred amid a ceremony of great pomp in the family vault at Fotheringhay, where they remain.

Edward may have chosen to be lenient to the city of York, but he was ruthless when it came to his noble enemies. The Earl of Devon had been captured in the pursuit after the battle. His earlier brutality and lack of honesty now caught up with him for on 3 April he was beheaded in public. He was followed by another 32 prisoners. Edward tended to prefer leniency to execution, but he despised men who having been pardoned once then went back on their word.

Edward was disappointed to find that his rival monarch, Henry VI, had fled along with his family and that nobody knew where they had gone. They had ridden north with a small escort as soon as news of the battle's result reached York, and had seemingly vanished off the face of the earth a few miles to the north. Somerset was also missing and as word of the cataclysmic defeat spread through England numerous other Lancastrian nobles dropped out of sight.

Edward sent scouts out across northern England, seeking to find the fugitives. Always they were one step ahead. At Carham Henry, Margaret and the young Edward were nearly caught, but they managed to slip out through a side postern gate as Edward's men rode in the front gate. They eventually escaped to Scotland, where they found temporary safety. Somerset joined them there later in 1461, as did many other Lancastrian nobles and knights.

One Lancastrian could not be found at all. This was Henry Clifford, the seven year old heir to the notorious Baron Clifford. When news of his father's death reached the family seat of Skipton Castle young Henry left the castle accompanied only by one woman servant. Edward searched for the boy everywhere, as did Lancastrian agents, but he was nowhere to be found and nobody would admit to knowing anything about him. It was not until 25 years later, after the last Yorkist king had been killed at the Battle of Bosworth and Henry Tudor sat on the throne of England, that Henry Clifford walked up to the gates of Skipton Castle and demanded both entrance and his lands back. He had spent the intervening years at Threlkeld in Cumberland where he had been working as a shepherd on the estates of an old family friend. Henry Tudor gave Henry his lands back, together with his titles. The new Baron Clifford was known for the rest of his life as the Shepherd Lord. He lived until 1523, dying peacefully at home.

Once he learned that Henry VI was in Scotland and so beyond his reach, Edward disbanded most of his army and travelled back to London. He was crowned King of England on 28 June and began a reign that would see England become more prosperous than it had been for generations. His understanding of merchants and business was legendary. His willingness to embrace new ideas and new ways of government made him unique among England's medieval kings and

The tomb of Lord Dacre stands in Saxton churchyard. His family insisted that he had to be buried upright sitting astride his warhorse, also upright. His tomb is therefore one of the most unusual in England.

paved the way for a new style of monarchy.

Edward remained secure on his throne until he fell out with the Earl of Warwick in 1470. Warwick's rebellion saw Edward flee abroad, but he was soon back to slay Warwick at the Battle of Barnet and so to re-establish himself on the throne until his death in 1483.

Henry VI was not so lucky. After staying for some time in Scotland he was brought back to England by Somerset in an effort to rally Lancastrian support, but was captured by Edward's men and taken to London. He was given comfortable lodgings in the Tower of London where he was free to enjoy his passions for music, arts and religion attended by servants befitting his new status as a nobleman. He died on 22 May 1471, officially from a fit of depression after hearing the news of the death of his son at the Battle of Tewkesbury. Most historians believe that he was murdered either by Edward or by his younger brother Richard - later King Richard III.

The Earl of Warwick who had done so much to put Edward on to the throne expected to be rewarded richly for his efforts. He was, indeed, given great wealth, but not the political power that he craved. He fell out with Edward over the choice of a bride for the new king and after several disputes raised a rebellion in 1470. Warwick's allies in the rising were Margaret of Anjou and her son Edward, with Henry VI as figurehead. Warwick was at first successful, but was in 1471 defeated and killed at the Battle of Barnet by Edward, who then marched on to defeat and kill young Prince Edward at the Battle of Tewkesbury a few weeks later.

The Duke of Somerset escaped to Scotland, then travelled in France and Flanders before returning to England to make his peace with Edward IV. Edward allowed him to keep his estates and titles in return for a promise of loyalty, which Somerset made. In early 1463, however, Somerset raised a rebellion against Edward IV. That rising ended in total defeat at the Battle of Hexham. Somerset was captured and, having broken his vows of loyalty, was executed. He was buried in Hexham Abbey and his helmet is on display in Hexham Museum.

William Neville, Baron Fauconberg, was richly rewarded for his decisive action at Towton by Edward. He was made Earl of Kent and granted 46 manors to add to his already impressive estates. He spent the following months patrolling Lancastrian areas and installing garrisons at likely troublespots. He died unexpectedly on 9 January 1463 at the age of 58. He was buried in Guisborough Abbey, his tomb being destroyed during the Reformation.

After having fallen ill during the Towton campaign, the Duke of Norfolk never really recovered. He managed to perform his duties as Earl Marshal during the coronation of Edward, but then retired to his estates where he died on 6 November 1461. He was buried at Thetford Priory and his tomb destroyed during the Reformation.

Back on the battlefield, the elder tree from which was fired the crossbow bolt that killed Lord Dacre became something of a tourist attraction. Many people using the Great North Road made the short diversion to view the tree. The tree died in the 18th century, but seeds from it were replanted on the spot and three new elders grow there today. A living reminder of the bloodiest battle ever fought in England.

ALSO AVAILABLE IN THIS SERIES

The Battle of Wimbledon 568
The Battle of Crug Mawr 1136
The Battle of Lincoln 1141
The Battle of Lewes 1264
The Battle of Chesterfield 1266
The Battle of Bannockburn 1314
The Battle of Brighton 1377
The Battle of Northampton 1460
The Battle of Towton 1461
The Battle of Losecoat Field 1470
The Battle of Bosworth 1485
The Sieges of Newark 1643-46
The Siege of Leicester 1645